W9-DDG-331

Dear Friend of Truth in Action Ministries,

Thank you for requesting this important booklet. What you are about to read will surprise, shock, and anger you. I hope it moves you to action.

It is the story—in brief—of the "gay agenda's" stunning progress over the last 40 years.

It is a moral revolution that we at Truth in Action Ministries saw coming—and one which we have worked hard to oppose. Nearly 20 years ago, homosexuals marched outside Coral Ridge Presbyterian Church, waving placards that accused its pastor, Dr. D. James Kennedy, my late father, of "hate" and linking him to the Ku Klux Klan. Those kinds of accusations are now standard fare against anyone who says it is wrong to engage in same-sex intercourse or declares that the Bible opposes "marriage" between members of the same gender.

The well-rehearsed practice of pushing what author Michael Brown calls the "hate button" is part of a brilliant public relations strategy to turn moral and biblical objections to homosexual conduct into expressions of bigotry and "hate." That strategy has worked exceptionally well. Very few voices in American culture are now raised against homosexual conduct. And even while opposition to homosexuality has been cowed, homosexual forces have invaded America's public schools and are re-educating our nation's young people, starting in some cases in kindergarten, to believe that "gay is okay"—and not just okay, but something to be celebrated and supported.

God Himself has been enlisted by homosexual activists in what can only be described as a blasphemous distortion of biblical truth. Instead of the plain and easily ascertained truth that the scriptures condemn homosexual conduct as an abhorrent sin, theological apologists for homosexual license have reinvented biblical morality to turn homosexuality into something holy and good. We are told, for example, that David and Jonathan were homosexual lovers, as were Naomi and Ruth, and, most blasphemously, Jesus and John, the "beloved apostle."

The homosexual revolution through which we have lived is not about tolerance. Where they have achieved power, homosexuals no longer allow dissent. Dr. Brown presents disturbing accounts of the severe reaction visited on those who dare to disagree.

This short excerpt, pulled from Dr. Brown's nearly 700-page volume, reveals the threat to America's moral health, the innocence of children, biblical truth, and religious liberty now bearing down on us from the gay agenda. We have removed endnote documentation from this condensed adaptation due to space restrictions, but rest assured, Dr. Brown has done his homework. His original work, *A Queer Thing Happened to America: And what a long, strange trip it's been*, includes some 90 pages of endnotes, and is available from Truth in Action Ministries when you visit www.TruthInAction.org.

We are grateful for your friendship, support, and prayers on our behalf as we, together, stand for biblical truth and reach out with the love and redemption found only in Christ.

Sincerely in Christ,

Jennifer Kennedy Cassidy

Jennifer Kennedy Cassidy
Member, Board of Directors

A STEALTH AGENDA

MICHAEL L. BROWN

Truth in Action Ministries
P.O. Box 1
Fort Lauderdale, FL 33302
www.TruthInAction.org

ISBN: 978-1-929626-50-2

Printed in the United States of America

A STEALTH AGENDA

CONTENTS

The "Gay Agenda" is but one of the many lies promulgated
by radical religious political activists.

THE RAINBOW ALLIANCE

The "gay agenda" is a term that has been coined for propaganda pur-
poses by the forces of religious fundamentalism. To enhance what they
would have others believe is the ominous dimension of this term, they
also refer to "the homosexual agenda."

JACK NICHOLS, THE GAY AGENDA

There is no "Gay Agenda." Stop mentioning this phantom
of the Religious Right. There are those people who care about
civil rights and those who do not. That is all. Nobody is trying to take
over the world, nobody wants "special rights," and nobody
is trying to warp Western society to suit his or her individual needs....
This is not a conspiracy.

POSTED BY "MAYHEMYSTIC" ON PLASTIC.COM

THERE IS NO GAY AGENDA
Gays are just as much of a mixed bag as the rest of you nuts.

POSTED ON THE PRO GAY-MARRIAGE WEBSITE PRYHILLS: LIVING IN WHOLLY MATRIMONY

Repeat after me: There is no homosexual agenda. There is no
homosexual agenda. There is no homosexual agenda.

POSTED BY "HADANELITH" ON FSTDT.COM

CHAPTER 1

A Stealth Agenda

Is there really a homosexual agenda? Is there truly an insidious gay plot to undermine traditional values and subvert the American family? The very idea of it appears to be laughable — especially to the gay and lesbian community. Consider this anonymous, widely-circulated posting:

The Gay Agenda (Author Unknown)

I know that many of you have heard Pat Robertson, Jerry Falwell and others speak of the "Homosexual Agenda," but no one has ever seen a copy of it. Well, I have finally obtained a copy directly from the Head Homosexual. It follows below:

6:00 am	Gym
8:00 am	Breakfast (oatmeal and egg whites)
9:00 am	Hair appointment
10:00 am	Shopping
12:00 pm	Brunch

2:00 pm
1) Assume complete control of the U.S. Federal, State and Local Governments as well as all other national governments,
2) Recruit all straight youngsters to our debauched lifestyle,
3) Destroy all healthy heterosexual marriages,
4) Replace all school counselors in grades

> K-12 with agents of Colombian and Jamaican drug cartels,
>
> 5) Establish planetary chain of homo breeding gulags where over-medicated imprisoned straight women are turned into artificially impregnated baby factories to produce prepubescent love slaves for our devotedly pederastic gay leadership,
>
> 6) Bulldoze all houses of worship, and
>
> 7) Secure total control of the Internet and all mass media for the exclusive use of child pornographers.
>
> **2:30 pm** Get forty winks of beauty rest to prevent facial wrinkles from stress of world conquest
>
> **4:00 pm** Cocktails
>
> **6:00 pm** Light Dinner (soup, salad, with chardonnay)
>
> **8:00 pm** Theater
>
> **11:00 pm** Bed (du jour)

A gay agenda? What a joke! Simply stated, a "gay agenda" does not exist anymore than a "Head Homosexual" exists — at least, that's what many gays and lesbians would surely (and sincerely) say.

As expressed by the widely-read, lesbian blogger Pam Spaulding, "The Homosexual Agenda is an elusive document. We've been looking around for a copy for quite some time; the distribution plan is so secret that it's almost like we need a queer Indiana Jones to hunt the master copy down. The various anti-gay forces are certain that we all have a copy and are coordinating a[n] attack to achieve world domination." Right!

This much is sure: Despite the fact that the "homosexual community" is as diverse as the "heterosexual community," there is vast agreement among homosexuals that there is no such thing as a gay agenda. In fact, such terminology is to be studiously avoided, as noted by GLAAD (the Gay & Lesbian Alliance Against Defamation) in its informational posting "Offensive Terminology to Avoid":

OFFENSIVE: "gay agenda" or "homosexual agenda"
PREFERRED: "lesbian and gay civil rights movement"
or "lesbian and gay movement"

Lesbians and gay men are as diverse in our political beliefs as other communities. Our commitment to equal rights is one we share with civil rights advocates who are not necessarily lesbian or gay. "Lesbian and gay movement" accurately describes the historical effort to achieve understanding and equal treatment for gays and lesbians. Notions of a "homosexual agenda" are rhetorical inventions of anti-gay extremists seeking to portray as sinister the lesbian and gay civil rights movement.

There you have it, straight from an authoritative source: "Notions of a 'homosexual agenda' are rhetorical inventions of anti-gay extremists seeking to portray as sinister the lesbian and gay civil rights movement." Thus, there are no facts behind this claim, only notions; there is no substance to this charge only rhetorical inventions; those behind these accusations are not balanced, well-meaning people but rather anti-gay extremists; the movement in question is nothing less than a civil rights movement, and the only thing sinister about this movement is the way it is portrayed by the fanatical opposition.

So then, the "gay agenda" is a myth? The testimony is unanimous and unequivocal: there is no gay agenda. Case closed. Or is it?

IS THERE MORE TO THE STORY?

Carl Wittman's landmark *Refugees from Amerika: Gay Manifesto*, dated Thursday, January 1, 1970, concluded with **AN OUTLINE OF IMPERATIVES FOR GAY LIBERATION**:

1. Free ourselves: come out everywhere; initiate self defense and political activity; initiate counter community institutions.
2. Turn other gay people on: talk all the time; understand, forgive, accept.

3. Free the homosexual in everyone: we'll be getting a
good bit of [expletive] from threatened latents: be
gentle, and keep talking & acting free.

4. We've been playing an act for a long time, so we're
consummate actors. Now we can begin to be, and it'll
be a good show!

But there is no gay agenda, despite a gay manifesto with a call to
action for the purpose of gay liberation.

Literature distributed at the 1987 March on Washington listed
seven major demands, including the legal recognition of lesbian
and gay relationships and the repeal of all laws that make sodomy
between consenting adults a crime, while the 1993 event was billed
as the March on Washington for Lesbian, Gay, and Bi Equal Rights and
Liberation. The opening item in the Platform Demands stated: "We
demand passage of a Lesbian, Gay, Bisexual, and Transgender civil
rights bill and an end to discrimination by state and federal governments including the military; repeal of all sodomy laws and other laws
that criminalize private sexual expression between consenting adults."
The third Platform Demand stated: "We demand legislation to prevent
discrimination against Lesbians, Gays, Bisexuals and Transgendered
people in the areas of family diversity, custody, adoption and foster
care and that the definition of family includes the full diversity of all
family structures." *But there is no gay agenda!*

In their pioneering 1990 volume *After the Ball: How America Will
Conquer Its Fear and Hatred of Gays in the 1990s*, Harvard-trained
gay authors Marshall Kirk and Hunter Madsen offered a brilliant and
comprehensive strategy for changing America's attitudes towards
homosexuality, as indicated by the subtitle, *How America Will Conquer Its Fear and Hatred of Gays in the '90s*. The book has been
referred to many times in the last two decades, especially by conserva-
tives who have noted how successful this plan has been.

This national #1 bestselling volume, which candidly speaks of "the
gay revolution," actually proposed "a practical agenda for bringing to a

close, at long last, the seemingly permanent crisis of American homo-sexuality." In fact, the authors even stated that, "In February 1988... a 'war conference' of 175 leading gay activists, representing organizations from across the land, convened in Warrenton, Virginia, to establish a four-point agenda for the gay movement" — *but there is no gay agenda*.

On January 13, 2005, twenty-two national gay and lesbian organiza-tions released a joint statement of purpose with eight goals, according to an article on GayPeoplesChronicle.com noting that, "The 22 organi-zations signing the document include just about all of the major nation-al LGBT [Lesbian, Gay, Bisexual, Transgender] groups." The statement itself observed that, "The speed with which our movement is advancing on all fronts is absolutely historic. We are born into families as diverse as our nation.... We, literally, are everywhere. " The eight goals were:

- Equal employment opportunity, benefits and protections
- Ending anti-LGBT violence
- HIV and AIDS advocacy, better access to health care, and LGBT-inclusive sex education
- Safe schools
- Family laws that strengthen LGBT families
- Ending the military's gay ban
- Exposing the radical right's anti-LGBT agenda and fight-ing their attempts to enshrine anti-gay bigotry in state and federal constitutions
- Marriage equality

The article reporting this on GayPeoplesChronicle.com was entitled "The Gay Agenda" — *but there is no gay agenda*.

The Human Rights Campaign (HRC), founded in 1980 and described on its website as "America's largest gay and lesbian organiza-tion," provides "a national voice on gay and lesbian issues. The Human Rights Campaign effectively lobbies Congress; mobilizes grassroots action in diverse communities; invests strategically to elect a fair-mind-ed Congress; and increases public understanding through innovative education and communication strategies." And it does all this with an annual budget of more than $35 million and a staff of more than 110. And for three years, Joe Solmonese, the president of the HRC, hosted a radio show called "The Agenda." *But there is no gay agenda.*

The National Gay and Lesbian Task Force (NGLTF), founded in 1974, and with an annual income in excess of $3.5 million, "works to build the grassroots political power of the LGBT [Lesbian, Gay, Bisexual, Transgender] community to win complete equality. We do this through direct and grassroots lobbying to defeat anti-LGBT ballot initiatives and legislation and pass pro-LGBT legislation and other measures." In addition to this, the Task Force has an organizing and training program, a policy institute, and an annual "Creating Change" conference. *But there is no gay agenda.*

The mission statement of Lambda Legal, with an income of better than $10 million annually, explains: "Lambda Legal is a national organization committed to achieving full recognition of the civil rights of lesbians, gay men, bisexuals, transgender people and those with HIV through impact litigation, education, and public policy work." In an oft-quoted statement, Paula Ettelbrick, the former legal director of the Lambda Legal Defense and Education Fund, once said, "Being queer is more than setting up house, sleeping with a person of the same gender, and seeking state approval for doing so. … Being queer means pushing the parameters of sex, sexuality, and family, and in the process transforming the very fabric of society." *But there is no gay agenda.*

Working in the educational system is GLSEN (pronounced "glisten"), with an annual budget of almost $6 million. Its mission statement explains: "The Gay, Lesbian and Straight Education Network strives to assure that each member of every school community is valued and respected regardless of sexual orientation or gender identity/expression." This includes training teachers in what is called "gender speak," recommending textbooks such as the famous (or, infamous) *Heather Has Two Mommies*, encouraging children to question their parents' non-gay-affirming views, and sponsoring an annual "Day of Silence" to draw attention to what is referred to as the widespread oppression and persecution of gays and lesbians — *but there is no gay agenda.*

The mission statement of GLAAD, whose own annual budget exceeds $4 million, states: "The Gay & Lesbian Alliance Against Defamation (GLAAD) is dedicated to promoting and ensuring fair, accurate and inclusive representation of people and events in the media as a means of eliminating homophobia and discrimination based on gender identity and sexual orientation." *But there is no gay agenda.*

So, there are well-funded, highly-motivated, sharply-focused gay activist organizations such as HRC and NGLTF and GLSEN and GLAAD and Lambda Legal — just to mention a few — *but there is no gay agenda.*

WHY DENY THE EXISTENCE OF A GAY AGENDA?

What is behind this consistent and concerted denial of a gay agenda?

Why is there such a unified gay denial of such an obvious gay agenda? Why the claim, quoted above, that, "Notions of a 'homosexual agenda' are rhetorical inventions of anti-gay extremists seeking to portray as sinister the lesbian and gay civil rights movement"? Why not state that the so-called gay and lesbian civil rights movement has a definite agenda? Why not articulate what this agenda includes?

Perhaps, some might argue, the real issue is that this so-called agenda is really not an agenda at all. Perhaps the reason for the consistent gay denial of a gay agenda is that the extent of that agenda is simply: Please leave us alone and let us live our lives in peace.

I beg to differ. That is not the only thing all the gay organizations and individuals are fighting for. To the contrary, the legitimizing of homosexuality as a perfectly normal alternative to heterosexuality also requires that all opposition to homosexual behavior must be delegitimized. At the very least, the gay agenda requires this (and let recognized gay leaders renounce this if it is not so):

- Whereas homosexuality was once considered a pathological disorder, from here on those who do not affirm homosexuality will be deemed homophobic, perhaps themselves suffering from a pathological disorder.

- Whereas gay sexual behavior was once considered morally wrong, from here on public condemnation — or even public criticism — of that behavior will be considered morally wrong.
- Whereas identifying as transgender was once considered abnormal by society, causing one to be marginalized, from here on those who do not accept transgenderism will be considered abnormal and will be marginalized.

IMPLICATIONS OF THE GAY AGENDA

This is all part of the mainstream gay agenda, a necessary corollary to the call for "gay and lesbian civil rights." In keeping with this:

- When the father of a six year-old child in Lexington, Massachusetts, notified his son's school that he wanted prior notification if anything related to homosexuality was to be taught in his son's first-grade class, he was rebuffed by the superintendent of schools who informed him that the court had ruled that it was more important to teach "diversity" — with specific reference to homosexuality — than to honor the requests of the parents. So much for parental rights!
- A Christian leader in Pennsylvania was charged with "Disorderly Conduct" and "Disrupting Meetings and Processions" for trying to read a passage from the New Testament that dealt with homosexual practices during his designated speaking time at a city council meeting. (He was actually shut down before he could read the passage.) Assistant District Attorney Alyssa Kunsturiss explained that the borough president "perceived what he was reading as hate speech. It would be homophobic today. They couldn't let him go on. You can't go up to the podium and start reading from the Bible." Yes, this is an accurate quote from an attorney right here in America, supposedly "one nation under God" and the home of free speech — as long as that speech does not challenge or differ with the gay agenda.
- In Boise, Idaho, an employee of Hewlett Packard was fired for posting Bible verses on his cubicle after a pro-gay poster was placed near

his workspace. According to the Ninth Circuit Court of Appeals, "An employer need not accommodate an employee's religious beliefs if doing so would result in discrimination against his co-workers or deprive them of contractual or other statutory rights."

- The Associate Vice President of Human Resources at the University of Toledo, an African American woman, was fired from her job "for stating in a guest column in a local newspaper that choosing homosexual behavior is not the same as being black or handicapped." The university president stood behind the decision to dismiss her.

Shockingly, the examples just cited are only the tiny tip of a massive iceberg. Here are just a few more. Were you aware of things such as:

- A "reeducation class" to ensure that foster parents embrace the gay agenda (California)?
- Public schools with a mandated pro-homosexual ["antidiscrimination"] policy that sends objecting students to "appropriate counseling" without notifying their parents (California)?
- Being put out of business (with a $150,000 fine) for firing a man in a dress (California)?
- Being told by a judge that you can't teach your daughter anything "homophobic" (Colorado)?

THE INEVITABLE PROGRESSION OF GAY ACTIVISM

All this is part of an inevitable process which can be summarized with this progression:

First, gay activists came out of the closet;
Second, they demanded their "rights";
Third, they demanded that everyone recognize those "rights";
Fourth, they want to strip away the rights of those who
    oppose them;
Fifth, they want to put those who oppose their "rights"
    into the closet.

As stated explicitly by GLSEN founder Kevin Jennings, "Ex-gay messages have no place in our nation's public schools. A line has been drawn. There is no 'other side' when you're talking about lesbian, gay and bisexual students."

It would appear, then, that "civil rights" for some means "limited rights" for others, and that by specific design. As stated explicitly in a teacher's lesson aid published by the Gay and Lesbian Educators [GALE] of British Columbia: "We must dishonour the prevailing belief that heterosexuality is the only acceptable orientation even though that would mean dishonouring the religious beliefs of Christians, Jews, Muslims, etc." All this is part of the gay agenda.

Does this surprise you? If so, bear in mind that these are not predictions. They are statements of fact, a recap of what has already taken place in America and what is currently taking place in Canada. Even our vocabulary is being affected, as the gay agenda has produced these new definitions and concepts:

- From here on, embracing diversity refers to embracing all kinds of sexual orientation, (homo)sexual expression, and gender identification but rejects every kind of religious or moral conviction that does not embrace these orientations, expressions, and identifications.

- From here on, tolerance refers to the complete acceptance of GLBT lifestyles and ideology — in the family, in the work place, in education, in media, in religion — while at the same time refusing to tolerate any view that is contrary.

- From here on, inclusion refers to working with, supporting, sponsoring, and encouraging gay events, gay goals while at the same time systematically refusing to work with and excluding anyone who is not in harmony with these events and goals.

- From here on, hate refers to any attitude, thought, or word that differs with the gay agenda, while gays are virtually exempt from the charge of hate speech — no matter how vile and incendiary the rhetoric — since they are always the (perceived) victims and never the victimizers.

In the last four decades, major changes have taken place in: 1) the public's perception of homosexuality and same-sex relationships; 2) the educational system's embrace of homosexuality; 3) legislative decisions recognizing gays and lesbians as a distinct group of people within our society, equivalent to other ethnic groups; 4) the media's portrayal of GLBT people; and 5) corporate America's welcoming of what was once considered unacceptable behavior. Is this simply one big coincidence? Did all this happen by chance? Don't these very results — which barely tell the story — give evidence to a clearly defined gay agenda?

Well, just in case you're not 100% sure, a leading gay activist has helped remove all doubt. Speaking shortly after the 2006 elections, Matt Foreman, then the executive director of the National Gay and Lesbian Task Force, had this to say:

> "You want to know the state of our movement on November 10, 2006? We are strong, unbowed, unbeaten, vibrant, energized and ready to kick some butt."

And what exactly does this mean? "The agenda and vision that we must proudly articulate is that yes, indeed, we intend to change society."

So, the cat is out of the bag and the covert agenda is becoming overt. It is nothing less than a gay revolution — and it is coming to a school or court or business or house of worship near you.

America, are you ready?

Liberty Counsel [an evangelical Christian legal organization] is a distinctly un-Christian, hate-filled intolerant gang of thugs with law degrees.

FROM AN EDITORIAL IN *Q-NOTES*, THE GAY NEWSPAPER OF THE CAROLINAS

The homo-hatred of the religious right has driven so many beautifully-gifted women and men into the arms of suicide, alcoholism, promiscuity, and self-destruction.

PASTOR MIKE PIAZZA, *HOLY HOMOSEXUALS*

A garden of homophobia: our black churches are fertile soils for planting and cultivating homo hatred.

ARTICLE IN THE *ADVOCATE* BY IRENE MONROE

You, just like everyone who is against gay marriage, is a mentally retarded bigot. No exceptions. Now go to hell.

WIZZYBOY 520, RESPONDING TO A YOUTUBE VIDEO *BY A TWELVE-YEAR-OLD BOY WHO OPPOSED SAME-SEX MARRIAGE BASED ON THE BIBLE*

… the charge of "hate" is not a contribution to argument; it's the recourse of people who would rather not have an argument at all.

MATTHEW J. FRANCK, *THE WASHINGTON POST*
DECEMBER 19, 2010

Jewish Hitlers, Christian Jihadists, and the Magical Effects of Pushing the "Hate" Button

No one likes being manipulated. No one enjoys being used as a pawn. Yet psychological manipulation has taken place on a massive scale in our country, and it's as simple as pushing a one word button. Yes, the moment the button is pushed, clear-minded, rational thinking virtually ceases and people respond with one accord, as if on cue.

What makes this all the more striking is that it was scripted out twenty years ago when two Harvard-trained, gay authors, Marshall Kirk and Hunter Madsen, published their watershed book After the Ball: How America Will Conquer Its Fear and Hatred of Gays in the '90s. Their goal was the "conversion of the average American's emotions, mind, and will, through a planned psychological attack, in the form of propaganda fed to the nation via the media."

One of their strategies was to "jam" people's emotions by associating "homo-hatred" with Nazi horror, bringing to mind images such as "Klansmen demanding that gays be slaughtered," "hysterical backwoods preachers," "menacing punks," and "a tour of Nazi concentration camps where homosexuals were tortured and gassed."

The strategy has worked like a charm, as Jeff Jacoby, a conservative columnist with the Boston Globe, noted, "Dare to suggest that homosexuality may not be something to celebrate and you instantly

19

are a Nazi. ... Offer to share your teachings of Christianity or Judaism with students 'struggling with homosexuality' and you become as vile as a Ku Kluxer...." Or, in the words of Dr. Laura Schlessinger, "Simply because I am opposed to legislating homosexual marriage and adoption, I am labeled a Nazi."

So, two Jews, Jacoby and Schlessinger, can be called Nazis — without the slightest hint of irony — simply because they expressed their differences with the goals of homosexual activism. Yes, all you have to do is push that "hate button," and the results are utterly predictable.

Not that long ago, "to hate" meant: "to feel hostility or animosity toward; to detest." In recent years, however, the Contemporary Lexicon of Political Correctness and Sensitivity to Sexual Orientation has expanded this definition of "hate" to include: "to hold to Judeo-Christian principles and values; to stand for biblical morality," and, quite specifically, "to take issue with homosexual practice."

Pushing the hate button has proven quite effective, causing levelheaded, reasonable discourse to come to a sudden halt and quickly making the person with whom you differ into a small-minded, mean-spirited bigot. Immediately, the playing field becomes unequal, and your ideological opponent becomes a monster whose ideas are unworthy of serious consideration. And should that opponent happen to be a person with strong religious convictions, then pushing the hate button becomes all the more useful. The conservative Christian or Jew is caricatured as a modern day crusader, witch-hunter, and jihadist rolled into one, a self-righteous, insensitive hypocrite who gleefully consigns all but a few likeminded fanatics to eternity in hell.

To be sure, many homosexual men and women have been subjected to all kinds of abuse and, sadly, they often continue to be the objects of vicious and even violent hatred. Homophobia does exist, despite the extreme overuse of that word today, and in the strongest possible terms, I decry hateful acts and words directed against the gay and lesbian community.

But let's be candid here. Things have shifted so dramatically — they have literally been turned upside down — that it now appears that no matter what you say and no matter how carefully and graciously you say it, if you dare to differ with the GLBT agenda, if you believe that it is immoral for a man to have sex with another man, if you do not support same-sex marriage, then you are an extremist, a bigot, a Nazi, and a jihadist.

AN EXAMPLE OF GENUINE HATE SPEECH

This is not the slightest exaggeration. In fact, I can confirm this firsthand. But first, let's take a look at some real, hardcore, unabashed, hate speech by none other than Rev. Fred Phelps, considered by many to be one of the foremost practitioners of hate speech in our day. It seems that there is no end to the ire of Rev. Phelps, as he continues to spew bile and launch one hateful website after another, including, godhatesamerica.com, hatemongers.com, and, as expected, godhatesfags.com. Yes, it is homosexuals who are the special target of his wrath, as evidenced in his response to someone who dared question his use of the word "fags":

> Answer to a nit-picking freak who pretends not to understand why we call fags fags... I must say: GET A GRIP! GET A CLUE! These are filthy beasts, no matter what you call them! Those three letters don't change the fact that the Lord will shortly return to execute judgment on this evil, froward world — and you will have to give an accounting for your rebellion against the Lord your God (and your attempt at distracting the saints). God hates fags. You are going to hell. Have a lovely day.

This is hate speech, plain and simple, and without apology. Sadly, this is the attitude of some misguided people who seek to validate their venom through a bogus use of the Bible, and Phelps has gained national notoriety for his vitriolic campaign, perhaps most famously for his "God hates fags" placards and signs.

"FRED PHELPS MINUS THE COLORFUL SIGNS"?

You can imagine, then, that I was more than a little surprised when a young, Charlotte-based gay activist and newspaper editor, Matt Comer, referred to me and my organization, the Coalition of Conscience, as "Fred Phelps minus the colorful signs." To be sure, I was fully aware of the reflex reaction that immediately associates all opponents of homosexual activism with "hysterical backwoods preachers." But comparing the Coalition of Conscience to "Fred Phelps minus the colorful signs" — wasn't this a little over the top, especially given our track record in our city? In May 2006, we had issued a public statement in which we apologized to the gay and lesbian community of Charlotte for the shortcomings of the Church, saying in part:

> We recognize that we have sometimes failed to reach out to you with grace and compassion, that we have often been insensitive to your struggles, that we have driven some of you away rather than drawn you in, that we have added to your sense of rejection. For these failings of ours, we ask you to forgive us. By God's grace, we intend to be models of His love.

And in February 2007, when we held a five-night lecture series on "Homosexuality, the Church, and Society" at the Booth Playhouse of the Blumenthal Performing Arts Center in Charlotte, we went out of our way to air our differences with gay and lesbian activists respectfully. The *Charlotte Observer* even noted in a supportive editorial that I had stated clearly that the lectures would "not be 'a forum for gay bashing'" and that I would "do nothing that's 'bigoted or mean-spirited.'" All this was known to Matt Comer when he made the Phelps comparison.

In fact, on September 20, 2007, Matt attended a public forum we conducted at our church devoted to the theme, "Can You Be Gay and Christian?" We had invited local gay and gay-affirming clergy to present their views and have a public dialogue with us, assuring them that there would be no gay-bashing or hate speech permitted. Although those invited decided to boycott the event, Matt did come and, with our permission, videotaped the entire presentation for his blog, without restriction. I spent time with him before the meeting and then, later in the evening, after our presentations were over, we gave him the microphone and let him share his own personal story.

In the midst of his "testimony" he said something that was quite striking: "You had some very good points, and they were couched in very compassionate language, but for a person like me, throughout this whole thing, all I'm going to hear is 'the queers need to die.'"

How telling and how sad. To paraphrase: "No matter what you say, and no matter how compassionately you say it, I'm still going to hear hatred coming from your lips."

What an admission, and what a window of understanding into the whole question of "hate speech." Could it be that the "hate" is not so much on the lips of the speakers (with notable exceptions such as Fred Phelps) as much as it is in the ears of the hearers? And, to take this one step further, could it be that the tables have now turned so dramatically that most of the hate speech is coming from the lips and pens of those who perpetually push the hate button, namely, the gay and lesbian community?

In an editorial published in *Q-Notes*, the gay newspaper of the Carolinas, Matt wrote that I followed "a carefully plotted and scripted message of 'compassion,' 'love' and 'gentleness'" (in other words, he couldn't find fault with what I actually said in terms of my spirit and attitude), but in reality, I was a "predator," and a "wolf in sheep's clothing," while those who agreed with me were "fanatics." And to cap things off, the editorial featured a ridiculous, doctored photo of me depicted as a Muslim terrorist and meant to be fear-inciting.

There you have it: Michael Brown, Christian Jihadist, aka Fred Phelps minus the signs. It looks like Jeff Jacoby and Laura Schlessinger had it right after all!

THE HATED DR. DOBSON

Consider one of the most admired men — and hated men — in

America today, psychologist, author, radio host, and influential evangelical leader Dr. James Dobson. In his book *Marriage Under Fire*, he wrote:

> At the risk of being misunderstood, let me acknowledge
> that there is a great reservoir of hatred in the world, and
> some of it unfortunately gets directed toward homosexu-
> als. It is wrong and hurtful, but it does happen. Every
> human being is precious to God and is entitled to accep-
> tance and respect. Each of us has a right to be treated with
> the dignity that comes from being created in the image of
> God. I have no desire to add to the suffering that homo-
> sexuals are already experiencing. In fact, it has been my
> intention to help relieve suffering by clarifying its causes
> and pointing to a way out.

How would you characterize those words? Compassionate? Concerned? Caring? Without question, Dobson seems to go out of his
way to express his love for gay men and women. Yet he is consistently
charged with being hateful and homophobic. Why? Because he dares
to suggest that homosexual practice is wrong and that homosexuals
can potentially change, and therefore he is hateful. Are you surprised?

Hate speech? Certainly not by any rational criteria. Yet as quickly
as Dobson's name is mentioned in the context of homosexuality,
the hate button will be pushed. Here are a couple of representative
quotes from one online bulletin board:

> Mr. Dobson is just like the rest of the religious fanatics out
> there. He's been raised and educated in an environment
> that promotes ignorance and stupidity. An environment that
> bases their faith upon a book that is up to 85% incomplete
> and inaccurate (as do the large majority of Americans.)

> That Dobson is a manic homophobe is no surprise.

A student editor for a Decatur, Illinois college newspaper expressed similar sentiments:

> Hey conservative Christians! Why do so many of you hate Americans and other people and the entire world? Why do you pass judgment as though that's what you were put on earth to do? And why have you let Dr. James Dobson be a "moral leader" for the last twenty-seven years when he is clearly an irrational, insane homophobe on a quest from his hateful god to divide and destroy instead of unite and love? Come on, you can do better than that. You can have minds of your own!

Now, stop for a moment and ask yourself a question: Who here is guilty of hate speech, Dr. Dobson or his critics? Whose rhetoric more closely resembles that of the aforementioned Fred Phelps? Who is guilty of name calling? Who is guilty of crass speech? Who is guilty of character defamation? Surely it is Dobson's critics.

In these few quotes alone, he was grouped with "religious fanatics," said to have "been raised and educated in an environment that promotes ignorance and stupidity" — does that include his postgraduate studies at UCLA? — called a "manic homophobe" and an "irrational, insane homophobe on a quest from his hateful god." Yet it is Dobson and his ideological colleagues who are labeled hate-filled. How utterly incongruous – and yet how marvelously effective. Pushing the hate button works wonders!

AN ANGRY LITTLE BOOK?

Psychiatrist and professor Jeffrey Satinover penned a very compassionate and yet forthright book called *Homosexuality and the Politics of Truth*. In the Introduction, he described in vivid detail how the subject of homosexuality first became a major focus in his life back in 1981. It was when he encountered his first AIDS victim (although the disease was not yet known by that acronym), a young man named

Paul. Satinonver spoke tenderly of him and "of his all-too-brief life and painful, wasting death," also stating that "AIDS was certainly unexpected and more horrifying than anyone could have imagined." And while he clearly expressed his opposition to certain aspects of gay activism, he also wrote, "How can our hearts not go out to the young, prehomosexual boy or girl who is already shy, lonely, sensitive, and who surely suffers taunting rejection and maybe even beatings by the very peers he or she envies and most longs to be with?"

Some reviewers on Amazon, however, were not impressed with Satinover's tone:

An angry little book full of error and distortion,

June 3, 2005

This book is quite ridiculous. My ex-boyfriend's mother gave it to him to read when he came out, thinking it might set him on the path to a "cure." Well, with the inexorable march of time, it was she who was "cured" of her misconceptions, prejudice etc. We can all look back and laugh at it now. So if anyone out there is having difficulty accepting the social fact of homosexuality, I would say to you — there is a better way forward. It involves accepting people's basic humanity, and the diversity of human experience. The alternative is the vile hatred espoused in a book like this. I think the world has well and truly moved on since it was published.

Why can't we give 0 stars!!, July 20, 2003

...I would suggest reading this book if you are a strict fundamentalist christian or have some particular hatred of gay people. If that describes you this book will make you feel more justified in your opinion and as long as you don't act on that opinion it's good to at least feel good about yourself, just be sure not to read any modern scientific studies on the subject because any study done in the last several decades by any of the most respected names in mental health easily

crush this book's weak evidence and show it to be nothing
more than an attempt to justify hatred.

Angry little book? Vile hatred? Some particular hatred of gay
people? An attempt to justify hatred? One reviewer, whose language
was fairly moderate — aside from calling the book "horrifying" —
wrote, "Although Satinover goes out of his way to present himself as
someone who genuinely cares about gay people and wants to help
them, he does not seem to acknowledge their role in their own lives,
preferring instead to see them as victims of their own nature."

Is it possible that he does, in fact, genuinely care, and it is that care
that motivated him to write the book? Is it so hateful to believe that
homosexual practice is harmful and that change is possible? (If a doctor takes issue with you or me being overweight, do we brand him or
her an anti-fat, hate-filled bigot, or do we recognize that the doctor is
expressing concern for our well-being? Isn't the doctor trying to be
helpful rather than hateful?)

It is one thing to disagree with Satinover's findings from a scientific viewpoint or from personal experience to deny that change is
possible. But why must the hate button be pushed incessantly? Are
the only two options "embracing homosexuality" or "hatred"?

At the end of a June 24, 2005, editorial in the *Charlotte Observer*, I
wrote: "If some still choose to push this emotionally charged button,
others can choose to make it ineffective by determining instead to
seek out and hear the truth, recognizing that whoever uses the rhetoric of 'hate' is most likely deflecting discussion from the real issues at
hand. And it is only through bringing the real issues into the light that
we can render the hate button obsolete. Isn't it time?"

I have made the personal determination never to push the hate button but rather to hear out those who differ with me? Will you join me?

*It is particularly important to begin to make
three- to five-year-olds aware of the range of families that exist in the
UK today; families with one mum, one mum and dad, two mums,
two dads, grandparents, adoptive parents, guardians etc.*

RECOMMENDATION FROM THE UK'S
NATIONAL UNION OF TEACHERS (NUT),
JULY 2006

*Restroom Accessibility: Students shall have access to the
restroom that corresponds to their gender identity exclusively
and consistently at school.*

OFFICIAL POLICY OF THE SAN FRANCISCO UNIFIED SCHOOL
DISTRICT SCHOOL BOARD (SFUSD)

*"Gender identity" refers to one's understanding, interests, outlook,
and feelings about whether one is female or male, or both, or neither,
regardless of one's biological sex.*

FROM THE LOS ANGELES UNIFIED SCHOOL
DISTRICT REFERENCE GUIDE

*Heterosexism: An overt or tacit bias against homosexuality rooted
in the belief that heterosexuality is superior or the norm.*

COMMON VOCABULARY REGARDING
SEXUAL ORIENTATION/GENDER IDENTITY
(FOR THE SFUSD)

Whoever captures the kids owns the future.

PATRICIA NELL WARREN, "FUTURE SHOCK," *THE ADVOCATE*, OCT 3, 1995.

CHAPTER 3

Boys Will Be Girls Will Be Boys: Undoing Gender and Teaching "Gay is Good" in Our Children's Schools

Moms and dads, boys and girls, it's time to read a special poem that I wrote just for you. It's called "Here at School the Slant Is Gay." Let's read out loud together on the count of three!

HERE AT SCHOOL THE SLANT IS GAY

Little Johnny went to school
There to learn a brand new rule;

No longer could the boys be boys
Or have their special trucks and toys;

Only six, so young and tender
It's time for him to unlearn gender

And break the binding two-sex mold
That hurtful thinking that's so old.

Parents at home can have their say
But here at school, the slant is gay.

In other words, to make this clear
There's nothing wrong with being queer.

Having two moms is mighty fine;
To disagree is out of line.

We'll deconstruct the family
And smash religious bigotry

And keep the church out of the state
By saying faith is really hate.

Free speech can only go one way,
Since here at school, the slant is gay.

So little ones, it's time to learn
'bout famous queers, each one in turn;

Lesbian greats long neglected
Well-known gays just now detected.

Some, perhaps, were man-boy lovers;
We'll keep that stuff under the covers.

GLSEN will fill in for Granny
And help kids find their inner-trannie.

Those born in a body that's wrong
Will hear of sex-change before long.

And through the years as Johnny grows
He will learn that anything goes.

With Bill, who's trans and Joe, who's bi-,
And Sue, who thinks that she's a guy.

United in the Day of Silence,
Joining the Gay Straight Alliance –

A queer new system rules the day,
Since here at school, the slant is gay.

Does this poem seem farfetched or exaggerated? Or does it strike you as a complete fabrication? If so, then you're in for a rude awakening. Welcome to the contemporary American school system. This is the day of the "queering of elementary education" — to quote the title of a highly-praised book — and much of this is due to the influence of GLSEN, the Gay, Lesbian, and Straight Educational Network.

MOMS AND DADS, MEET GLSEN

Celebrating their tenth anniversary in 2005, Kevin Jennings, GLSEN's founder and, at that time, Executive Director, was effusive:

One Decade Ago...

The education community was in profound denial about the very existence of LGBT students.

Fewer than a hundred gay-straight alliances existed. Fewer than 2 million students attended schools where harassment based on sexual orientation was prohibited. In short, just about nobody cared....

Today, ten years after we began our mission, more than 12 million students are protected by state laws. Nearly 3,000 schools have GSAs [Gay Student Alliances] or other student clubs that deal with LGBT issues. Over fifty national education and social justice organizations, including the National Education Association (NEA) have joined GLSEN in its work to create safe schools for our nation's children through projects like "No Name-Calling Week".

Then, after pointing out how much more work needed to be done, Jennings wrote:

GLSEN's tenth anniversary is a cause for celebration. It is a milestone for the organization, for the movement, and most importantly, for America's students. Let us take this joyous occasion to rededicate ourselves to the work of making our nation's schools places where young people learn to value and respect everyone, regardless of sexual orientation or gender identity/expression. The next generation deserves nothing less.

To be sure, some of GLSEN's goals are praiseworthy. I wholeheartedly agree with GLSEN that kids shouldn't pick on other kids because they seem to be different. But GLSEN's agenda goes far beyond this. GLSEN wants homosexuality and transgenderism completely normalized — and even encouraged, celebrated, and nurtured — in the educational system.

To put Jennings' ten-year statement in context, consider that by 1995, which was ground zero for GLSEN, dramatic changes had already taken place in our schools. In his book *School's Out: The Impact of Gay and Lesbian Issues on America's Schools*, Dan Woog expressed the seismic shift that had taken place from 1985 to 1995. For the sake of emphasis, I have inserted my comments in brackets:

A decade ago, who would have thought that an entire book could be written on the subject of homosexuality and education — written, in fact, using real names, real schools, and real incidents, many of them not only positive but spectacularly so? [Today, you could fill a small library with books like this.] Who would have thought that in so many buildings throughout the United States, in large cities, medium-sized suburbs, and tiny towns, there would be not only openly gay teachers, administrators, coaches, and students, but also gay-straight alliances, gay-themed curricula, and gay topics discussed honestly and intelligently in workshops, classes, and the pages of school newspapers? [And who would have thought that, from 1995 to 2010, these gay straight alliances would grow by more than 3000%?] It would have seemed like a fairy tale.

Today, in 2010, this hardly sounds like a fairy tale at all. In fact, it sounds rather ho-hum and commonplace. Gay-inspired curricula and gay-affirming educational programs are everywhere today, and according to GLSEN, from 1999-2007, Gay Straight Alliances in our schools have grown from 100 to 3,000.

What does seem like a fairy tale is that this scenario would have been unimaginable back in 1985. Today, that seems unthinkable. For gay educational activists, however, this is just the beginning, as expressed so clearly by Jennings.

THE GLSEN LUNCHBOX

What exactly, then, does this mean? And what precisely does GLSEN want to teach our children? Let's start with the GLSEN Lunchbox, an attractively packaged training tool for teachers beginning at kindergarten level, described as "A Comprehensive Training Program for Ending Anti-LGBT Bias in Schools." The GLSEN website states:

> The GLSEN Lunchbox 2 is a comprehensive training program aimed at providing educators and community members with the background knowledge, skills, and tools necessary to make schools safer and more affirming places for lesbian, gay, bisexual, and transgender (LGBT) students.

Does this sound innocent? Let's take a look inside.

The Lunchbox (which literally is a blue lunchbox), contains, among other items, a one-hour video, a "How to Use the GLSEN Lunchbox" manual, and a set of large cards outlining the format for each of the exercises, some of which address educators only, and some of which are for students of different ages. Outside of the lunchbox is a 141-page notebook binder, "The GLSEN Lunchbox Trainer's Manual."

Some of the activities include "North American History Game Cards," listing twenty-eight North Americans, most of whom are fairly well known and all of whom, according to GLSEN, are (or were) gay or transgender. (Among the better known names are Sara Josephine

Baker, James Baldwin, Leonard Bernstein, George Washington Carver, Babe Didrickson, Allen Ginsberg, Barbara Jordan, Margaret Mead, Harvey Milk, Bayard Rustin, Renee Richards, Andy Warhol, Walt Whitman, and Tennessee Williams.)

A similar game card activity is provided for World History, listing luminaries such as Alexander the Great, Hans Christian Anderson, Pope John XII, King Edward II, Noel Coward, Hadrian, Dag Hammserskjold, Joan of Arc, Elton John, Juvenal, Leonardo da Vinci, Michelangelo, Rudolph Nureyev, Pyotr Tchaikovsky, and Oscar Wilde. According to GLSEN, all of them were gay (or bisexual?).

The object of these activities is to help children and teachers recognize that many outstanding personalities in world and national history, including musicians, artists, statesmen, religious leaders, authors, and others, were gay. Therefore, being gay is neither negative nor bad nor degrading nor harmful nor dangerous.

Of course, a different set of conclusions could have been reached, namely, that until recently, these alleged homosexuals (or bisexuals) were content to function effectively and creatively in society without making a major issue of their sexuality — indeed, in a number of cases, the sexual orientation of these individuals is a matter of debate because they did not make an issue of their sexuality — and they were able to make important contributions to their generations and beyond without drawing attention to their sexual orientation.

There's also a dirty little secret that GLSEN will never mention, namely, that some of the men on this list were not just alleged homosexuals but alleged pederasts. As noted by Jim Kepner, formerly curator of the International Gay and Lesbian Archives in Los Angeles,

> if we reject the boylovers in our midst today we'd better stop waving the banner of the Ancient Greeks, of Michelangelo, Leonardo da Vinci, Oscar Wilde, Walt Whitman, Horatio Alger, and Shakespeare. We'd better stop claiming them as part of our heritage unless we are broadening our concept of what it means to be gay today.

I guess as far as famous pedophiles are concerned, GLSEN has adopted a "Don't ask, don't tell" policy. As we said in the poem, "We'll keep that stuff under the covers."

Some of these men cited in GLSEN's Lunchbox as being gay are cited by the North American Man-Boy Love Association (NAMBLA) as being pedophiles. In fact, according to NAMBLA, among the famous men listed in GLSEN's North American and World History Game Cards, Alexander the Great, Leonard Da Vinci, Michelangelo, and Oscar Wilde, were all "man-boy lovers." Thus, much of the alleged evidence for their homosexuality points specifically to pederasty. So, if they were practicing homosexuals, they were practicing pederasts. Should this be celebrated?

But there's more to the GLSEN lunchbox than queer history. It also seeks to strike at the very root of male-female distinctives. Thus, the activity called "Getting in Touch with Your Inner Trannie" (i.e., inner transgender identity) has as its stated purpose, "To help participants better understand and personally relate to the breadth of issues around gender identity and expression," asking the children questions such as: "Have you ever been told, 'Act like a lady/woman/girl,' or 'Act like a man?' What was the situation? How did it make you feel and why?" And, "If you see someone on the street whose gender is unclear to you, how do you react — both internally and externally?"

"THIS IS THE GENERATION THAT GETS IT"

Is it any wonder that GLSEN's Kevin Jennings, speaking of the wider goals of gay activism, told *Time Magazine*, "We're gonna win because of what's happening in high schools right now … this is the generation that gets it." And GLSEN and its allies are quite committed to being sure that today's school kids "get it." As expressed in "A Call to Action," issued in conjunction with the film, *It's Elementary: Talking about Gay Issues in School*:

> All teachers have the right, and the responsibility, to weave respectful, age-appropriate messages about LGBT people and issues into their lessons and classrooms. Educators should

not need to seek approval or have parental consent to discuss LGBT people and issues in the classroom in age-appropriate ways, unless the discussion involves actual sexual practices.

In light of all this, it is not surprising that the average age of kids "coming out" as homosexual has "dropped to 10 for gays and 12 for lesbians," according to the chair of Cornell University's human-development program — as if children of that age group have full clarity about their sexuality and the long-term consequences of the decisions they are making in this regard. But they are "coming out" earlier because: 1) clear gender definitions and distinctions are being "undone" and "deconstructed"; 2) they are getting indoctrinated about homosexuality and transgenderism; 3) they are being encouraged to "come out." And I remind you: This is happening in our public schools, supported by our tax dollars. How can this be?

In 1999, the respected publishing house of Rowman & Littlefield released the critically acclaimed volume *Queering Elementary Education: Advancing the Dialogue about Sexualities and Schooling*, edited by William J. Letts IV and James T. Sears. According to Prof. Debra Epstein of the Institute of Education, University of London, "Together and individually, the chapters of this book make a compelling case for queering elementary education, to the benefit of all children in all their diversity." Or, in the words of Prof. Peter McLaren, University of California-Los Angeles, "This volume marks the beginning of the queering of critical pedagogy and is long overdue."

So, the publication of this volume is a cause for celebration in the academic world. The time has arrived for the queering of elementary education. Really now, who would have thought we would live to see the day when the words "queering" and "elementary education" would be joined together?

And who would have thought that the joining of these words would produce jubilation among educators?

Chapters in this volume include:

• Teaching Queerly: Some Elementary Propositions

- Why Discuss Sexuality in Elementary School?
- Pestalozzi, Perversity, and the Pedagogy of Love
- Stonewall in the Housekeeping Area: Gay and Lesbian Issues in the Early Childhood Classroom
- Reading Queer Asian American Masculinities and Sexualities in Elementary School
- Using Music to Teach Against Homophobia
- "It's Okay to Be Gay": Interrupting Straight Thinking in the English Classroom
- Children of the Future Age: Lesbian and Gay Parents Talk about School
- Lesbian Mother and Lesbian Educator: An Integrative View of Affirming Sexual Diversity
- When Queer and Teacher Meet

Among scores of other books that could be mentioned are Arthur Lipkin's, *Understanding Homosexuality, Changing Schools: A Text for Teachers, Counselors, and Administrators*, which includes a chapter lauding "The Massachusetts Model" of LGBT education, and *Queer Theory in Education*, edited by William F. Pinar, with some of the most way-out and bizarre "educational" contributions imaginable.

NOT YOUR GRANDPARENTS' BEDTIME BOOKS

Dear parents, books like this are being used to train your children's educators, with many of these volumes serving as textbooks in colleges and universities. And what shall we say about the books that are being written for your children — or perhaps even being read to your children as early as pre-school? I'm talking about books like:

- *One Dad, Two Dads, Brown Dad, Blue Dads*, by Johnny Valentine. There is a special dedication at the beginning of the book, "To Jacob, who has only one mom and one dad. But don't feel sorry for him. They're both great parents." So, two dads are not just acceptable; two dads are now better than one dad and one mom. Extraordinary!

- Even more overt in its message is *Oh the Things Mommies Do! What Could Be Better Than Having Two?*, written by Crystal Tomkins with illustrations by "her wife" Lindsey Evans. The *Boston Spirit* magazine writes, "Given the physical and mental capacity available to one mom, it's hard to imagine that of two. Imagine even more phone calls 'to say Hi,' and exponentially more when you've got a cold or vocational hiccup." This is so much better than having one mom and one dad. (Really, what kind of physical and mental capacity does a dad have?)
- *Emma and Meesha My Boy: A Two Mom Story*, by Kaitlyn Considine, recommended for ages three-six.
- *Two Daddies and Me* by Robbie Ann Packard, who, "already a mother herself, had the amazing and joyous opportunity to become a surrogate for a gay couple."

May I ask you, current and prospective moms and dads, along with grandmas and grandpas, do you find books like this "reassuring"? Does it give you comfort to know that your kids might be reading through this book in school without your knowledge?

But it is not just GLSEN that is promoting these causes in our children's schools. The National Education Association (NEA) is an active, open, and proud co-conspirator. In 2009, the NEA released an official statement supporting same-sex marriage (which begs the question of why the National Education Association would be involved in this divisive political and moral issue at all). And in 2010, the NEA recognized a new caucus: the NEA Drag Queen Caucus.

Pause for a moment and wrap your mind around that: The National Education Association, which is the largest professional organization and labor union in the U.S., has recognized a drag queen caucus — and this is in addition to the already extant Gay & Lesbian, Bisexual and Transgender Caucus.

In 2003, Bob Chase, former president of the NEA, gave a glowing endorsement of GLSEN's *It's Elementary* training material, stating:

> Schools cannot be neutral when dealing with issues of
> human dignity and human rights [meaning, in particular,
> GLBT "dignity" and "rights"]. I'm not talking about toler-
> ance; I'm talking about acceptance.

But now "acceptance" is not enough. Homosexuality and other variant sexual orientations must be celebrated, as demonstrated by the Riddle Homophobia Scale, named after Dr. Dorothy Riddle and distributed and promoted by GLSEN for use in our schools. The scale lists four "Homophobic Levels of Attitude" and four "Positive Levels of Attitude."

Listed under the Homophobic category are: 1) Repulsion; 2) Pity; 3) Tolerance; and 4) Acceptance. That's correct: "Tolerance" and "Acceptance" are now considered homophobic! Listed under the Positive category are: 5) Support; 6) Admiration; 7) Appreciation; and 8) Nurturance.

Can you believe how much the tables have turned? For gay activists, it is not enough for our kids to tolerate or accept homosexuality. They must support and admire and appreciate and nurture it. (Shades of the children's books that presented same-sex households as superior to mom-and-dad households.)

As observed by Robert Weissberg, emeritus professor of political science at the University of Illinois-Urbana,

> Make no mistake, this is not just telling youngsters to
> ignore "odd" classmates, the traditional tolerance-based
> solution....Rather, this is a drive to legitimize homosexual-
> ity, swathed in the rhetoric of tolerance, by portraying this
> sexual predilection as "normal" at a time when youngsters
> barely grasp sexuality of any variety.

So... Little Johnny went to school, there to learn that queer was cool. Mom and Dad, what do you think of that?

Mary, Queer of Heaven and Mother of Faggots
Mary the drag queen (or is it Jesus cross-dressing?)

Two of the chapter titles in
Marcella Althaus-Reid's book *Indecent Theology*
(Althaus-Reid was Professor of Contextual Theology at the
New College, University of Edinburgh, Scotland)

"Do Not Be Conformed to This World":
Queer Reading and the Task of the Preacher

Title of the convocation address
at the Chicago Theological Seminary,
Dr. Ken Stone, September 15, 2004,
the 150th anniversary of the seminary
(Stone is the editor of *Queer Commentary*
and the Hebrew Bible)

Jesus is a boundary-breaker, transgressing the purity codes
of fundamentalists and challenging proto-heterosexual hegemony.

Rev. Robert E. Goss,
Writing in the *Queer Bible Commentary*

The Queer God is a call to 'disaffiliation' processes in theology.
To be unfaithful to sexual ideological constructions of God
in order to liberate God — a Queer God who also needs to
come out of the closet of theologians of the status quo.

Description of Marcella Althaus-Reid's book *The Queer God*,
posted on www.althaus-reid.com/QGodbook.html

CHAPTER 4

Queer Theology, a Gay/Lesbian Bible, and a Homoerotic Christ

WARNING: SOME OF THE MATERIAL IN THIS CHAPTER WILL BE EXTREMELY OFFENSIVE TO MANY READERS. LET THE READER PROCEED WITH CAUTION.

Rev. Prof. Peter J. Gomes is considered by many to be one of the foremost leaders in the African American Church, hailed also as one of the nation's most eloquent preachers. His resume is quite impressive, having served as the minister of Harvard University's Memorial Church and as Plummer Professor of Christian Morals at Harvard since 1974.

When he speaks, people listen, and so it is not surprising that he "was included in the summer 1999 premiere issue of *Talk Magazine* as part of its feature article, 'The Best Talkers in America: Fifty Big Mouths We Hope Will Never Shut Up.'"

Without a doubt, Rev. Prof. Gomes is a man of exceptional passion and dedication, and he is also an out of the closet, "gay Christian." Yes, the minister of Harvard's Memorial Church and the long-tenured Harvard professor of Christian morals is a homosexual, having come out in 1992 with his now famous statement, "I am a Christian who happens as well to be gay."

In his 1996 bestseller, *The Good Book: Reading the Bible with Heart and Mind*, Gomes devotes a whole chapter to "The Bible and Homosexuality," referring to the moral rejection of homosexual practice as a "biblically sanctioned prejudice." He writes:

> The legitimization of violence against homosexuals and
> Jews and women and blacks … comes from the view that
> the Bible stigmatizes these people, thereby making them
> fair game. If the Bible expresses such a prejudice, then it
> certainly cannot be wrong to act on that prejudice. This,
> of course, is the argument every anti-Semite and racist has
> used with demonstrably devastating consequences, as our
> social history all too vividly shows.

According to Gomes, it is fear that is "at the heart of homophobia, as it was at the heart of racism, and as with racism, religion — particularly the Protestant evangelical kind that had nourished me — [is] the moral fig leaf that covered prejudice." And it is this kind of prejudice, as Gomes and many other "homosexual Christians" argue, that has driven gays and lesbians out of the Church. This reflects a common theme in "gay Christian" literature: God loves us and accepts us as we are, but the Church closes its doors to us, judging us, rejecting us, and damning us to hell. Jesus takes us in, but the Church puts us out!

Certainly, in many ways, the Church has failed to reach out to the homosexual community, and, speaking personally as a leader in the Church, I am ashamed at the way we have often treated LGBT men and women. Many times, when reading their stories, especially those who experienced rejection and shunning by the Church, my heart has broken for them. Their pain is palpable, and their hurt anything but silent.

But does that mean it is time to rewrite the Bible? Because gays and lesbians have been hurt by the Church, must we now embrace queer theology? Must we create a homoerotic Christ and a gay God? Must we justify "gay Christianity"?

"But," you ask, "aren't there lots of different interpretations of the Bible? And isn't it true that even scholars disagree on what the Bible says about homosexuality?"

WHAT THE BIBLE REALLY SAYS ABOUT HOMOSEXUAL PRACTICE

As a biblical scholar, I'm sorely tempted to weigh in on these questions here and now, since the scriptural witness stands clearly and consistently against homosexual practice. As stated positively by Prof. Robert Gagnon, rightly regarded by many as today's foremost academic authority on the Bible and homosexual practice,

> Indeed, every narrative, law, proverb, exhortation, poetry, and metaphor in the pages of Scripture that has anything to do with sexual relations presupposes a male-female prerequisite for sexual relations and marriage.

The Bible really is quite clear about all this.

But this is not the time or place to discuss these questions, and there are a number of excellent books that address the issues in depth. Instead, let me share with you the inevitable direction in which "gay Christianity" develops.

Even for readers with little familiarity with the Bible — including readers who embrace other faiths — this will be of interest. Allow me, then, to introduce you to a brave, new — and increasingly queer — world, one that is sure to offend many a sensible reader.

Jesus taught that we could judge a tree by the fruit it produces. What kind of fruit does this "gay Christian" tree produce? In some respects, it resembles the traditional, biblical faith; in other respects, it is shockingly — and tellingly — different. Let's take an up close and personal look.

WHEN RELIGION BECOMES QUEER

The volume of collected essays entitled *Religion is a Queer Thing: A Guide to the Christian Faith for Lesbian, Gay, Bisexual and Transgendered People* is considered a mainstream book in "gay Christian" circles. In it, Elizabeth Stuart contributes a group lesson-guide and article on "The queer Christ," the aims of which are:

- to explore how traditional Christology was developed out of and reflects a context which has had negative repercussions for queer Christians;
- to explore some queer Christologies
- to encourage participants to reflect on their own understanding of Christ and bring it into critical dialogue with that of queer theologians and others in the group

More practical still are the prayers and liturgies collected by Stuart, including "A Rite of Repentance," in which the only sin that is addressed refers to "those times when we have denied God and the divine gift of our sexuality by pretending to know or understand nothing about homosexuality, bisexuality or transgender issues." Yes, repentance is offered for: "The times when we have smiled at and even joined in the anti-queer jokes for fear of being exposed as 'one of them.' The times when we have betrayed God our creator, ourselves, and our queer brothers and sisters by denying implicitly or explicitly that we are 'one of them.'"

There is also "A Liturgy for Coming Out":

> **The room should be darkened.**
> **The person coming out:** As Eve came out of Adam, as the people of Israel came out of slavery into freedom, as the exiled Israelites came out of Babylon back to their home, as Lazarus came out of the tomb to continue his life, as Jesus came out of death into new life I come out — out of the desert into the garden, out of the darkness into the light, out of exile into my home, out of lies into the truth, out of denial into affirmation. I name myself lesbian/gay/bisexual/transgendered. Blessed be God who has made me so.
> **All:** Blessed be God who made you so.
> *The person coming out lights a candle and all present light their candles from it. Flowers are brought in. Music*

is played. The whole room is gradually filled with light,
colour and music. Bread and wine are then shared.

So, Eve "coming out" of Adam, the Israelites "coming out" of Egypt
and Babylon, and Jesus and Lazarus "coming out" of the grave serve as
prototypes for gays and lesbians coming out of the closet? Indeed, some
of these themes are repeated in the writings of other queer theologians.

More striking still is a "Prayer of Thanks for our Bodies" written by
Chris Glaser. The first two stanzas read:

Thank you for the body that loves me.

My own body:
it tingles with pleasure
and sends me pain as a warning;
it takes in food and air
and transforms them to life;
it reaches orgasmic bliss
and reveals depths of peace.

Thank you for the body that loves me.

My lover's body [referring to a gay lover, of course]:
it surrounds me with safe arms,
and senses my needs and joys;
it allows me vulnerability,
and enables my ecstasy;
it teaches me how to love
and touches me with love.

Is it any wonder that a liturgical prayer celebrating "orgasmic bliss"
is found in a book entitled, *Coming Out to God: Prayers for Lesbians
and Gay Men, Their Families and Friends*? Have you found prayers
like this in the prayer book used by your religious tradition?

How about this stanza from a lesbian rendition of the Christmas carol "Silent Night," written in the midst of great spiritual and social struggles by Lucia Chappelle:

> *Silent night, raging night,*
> *Ne'er before, such a sight.*
> *Christian lesbians hand in hand.*
> *Many theories, one mighty band.*
> *Christ's new Body is born,*
> *Christ's new Body is born.*

Have you found this in any church hymnbook? It's found in the Metropolitan Community Church hymnal!

In the New Testament, Jesus told his followers that "where two or three come together in my name, there am I with them" (Matt 18:20). This statement seems to be fairly straightforward in meaning, unless, of course, you are reading the Bible through queer eyes, as is Prof. Kathy Rudy. In her article, "Where Two or More Are Gathered: Using Gay Communities as a Model for Christian Sexual Ethics," she applies the words of Jesus to random sexual encounters between gays:

> Each sexual encounter after that [in a bathroom or bar] shores up his membership in the community he finds there; and his participation and contribution subsequently makes the community he finds stronger for others. His identity begins to be defined by the people he meets in those spaces. Although he may not know the names of each of his sex partners, each encounter resignifies his belonging. And although no two members of the community make steadfast promises to any one person in the community, each in his own way promises himself as part of this world. Intimacy and faithfulness in sex are played out on the community rather than the individual level.

So, even anonymous sexual encounters with multiple partners, which reinforce the gay man's belonging to his community (and which, supposedly, and without a hint of irony, reflect "faithfulness in sex"), serve to exemplify what Jesus meant when he said, "where two or three come together in my name, there am I with them." This is put forth as serious theology.

REWRITING THE BIBLE IN THE IMAGE OF HOMOSEXUALITY

Yet a queer reading of the Bible goes farther still. It's as if everything is stood on its head and normal becomes abnormal. Indeed, the Bible is often understood and evaluated in light of homosexuality rather than homosexuality being understood and evaluated in light of the Bible. In other words, rather than asking, "What does the Bible teach us about homosexuality?" the question is, "What does homosexuality teach us about the Bible?"

In the section of *Religion Is a Queer Thing* entitled "Queer living: Ethics for ourselves, our societies and our world," John McMahon cites a 1991 article written by gay liberation theologian Rev. Dr. Robin H. Gorsline, "Let Us Bless Our Angels: A Feminist-Gay-Male-Liberation View of Sodom," in which Gorsline stated:

> Gay liberation is deeply suspicious of attempts, however well intentioned, to address the issue of homosexuality in the Bible. The issue is not of homosexuality and whether the Bible sustains, condemns, or is neutral about it. Neither canonical testament [i.e., neither the Old Testament nor the New Testament] carries any authority for gay liberation on the subject of homosexuality. Gay liberation interprets scripture, not the other way around.

Significantly, McMahon does not criticize this view, a view that for most Christians would be abhorrent. Instead, he simply raises a question for group discussion: "Do you think that the Bible has any place in discerning queer ethics? What do you make of Robin Gorsline's view that we enlighten scripture, rather than the other way around?"

What if a promiscuous heterosexual used this same approach, "enlightening" Scripture based on his sexual ethics? What if a sado-masochist did the same? (Again, I am not here equating homosexuals with sadomasochists or promiscuous heterosexuals; I am simply demonstrating the folly of claiming that we have the right to interpret the Bible based on our sexual orientation, choices, or behavior.)

And yet there is more: The Bible is actually reinterpreted — and sometimes even rewritten — in queer terms. Consider this example, also taken from McMahon's article. According to Mark 4:21-23, Jesus encouraged his followers to be unashamed of their faith, reminding them that, ultimately, everything would come to light:

> Is a lamp brought in to be put under the bushel basket, or under the bed, and not on the lampstand? For there is nothing hidden, except to be disclosed; nor is anything secret, except to come to light. Let anyone with ears to hear listen!

McMahon quotes this same text, adding the words in brackets. What a massive change a few words can make!

> Is a [queer] lamp brought in to be put under the bushel basket, or under the bed, and not on the lampstand? For there is nothing hidden [in the closet], except to be disclosed; nor is anything secret, except to come [out] to light. Let anyone with ears to hear listen!

According to McMahon's reinventing of the text, Jesus is now encouraging homosexuals to come out of the closet, reminding them that they have a queer lamp. So then, if the Bible doesn't say what you want it to, just add a few extra words, and voilà, there you have it.

GAYS AND LESBIANS EVERYWHERE

Here are some further examples of a "translesbigay" Bible. David and

Jonathan are commonly depicted as homosexual lovers, despite the fact
that David himself had numerous wives and concubines (see 2 Samuel
5:13), and despite the fact that his great, personal fall came as a result
of his adulterous lust for Bathsheba, whose husband David killed so he
could have her for himself (see 2 Samuel 11). So much for a gay David!

Sadly, the homosexual reading of Scripture seems unable to understand the extraordinarily close, non-sexual relationship that can exist
between two men (or two women), a type of relationship that was
more common and culturally accepted in many ancient cultures and a
relationship that remains common and culturally accepted in certain
parts of the world today — again, in totally non-sexual terms. Instead,
the gay reading of Scripture insists that these words of David, eulogiz-
ing Jonathan, must be interpreted in sexual terms:

> I grieve for you, Jonathan my brother;
> you were very dear to me.
> Your love for me was wonderful,
> more wonderful than that of women (2 Samuel 1:26).

So, Jonathan's love for David had to be sexual, despite the fact
that David, whom, I reiterate, was anything but gay according to the
Scriptures, referred to Jonathan as his brother, not his lover. Similarly,
because Naomi and her daughter-in-law Ruth were very close, they
must have been lesbian lovers (I kid you not!), despite the fact that
the Bible does not even give the slightest hint of this, and despite the
fact that both of them married and had children (Ruth even remar-
ried after she was widowed). So also Mary and Martha, the sisters of
Lazarus, whom Jesus raised from the dead, must also have been lesbian
spinsters. Otherwise, why were they not married and out of the house?
Come to think of it, why was Lazarus living at home too? He must have
been gay! Yes, all this has been put forth in "gay Christian" writing.

Even Perpetua and Felicity, martyred by the Romans in 203 and
known for their unshakable love for Jesus and their great devotion
for each other, must have been lesbian lovers — despite the fact that

Perpetua had a child and was married, and despite the fact that there is not a single syllable in any ancient Christian literature that suggested any same-sex interest between them — since the only deep love that can exist between people of the same sex must be sexual in nature. Thus the martyrs Perpetua and Felicity have been called "Queer saints."

Not surprisingly, whole books have been written on the alleged erotic relationship between Jesus and his disciple John, the one often called "the beloved disciple" because John spoke of Jesus' special love for him (see, e.g., John 21:20; for a representative study, see Theodore W. Jennings, Jr., *The Man Jesus Loved: Homoerotic Narratives from the New Testament*.) In this case too, however, the Bible makes no reference of any kind to any form of sexual or "homoerotic" relationship between Jesus and John, and so the question must be asked: Is it that hard to conceive that Jesus, the Son of God, especially cared for one of his disciples without that care having to be sexual? Must queer theology insist on "queering Christ"?

But this is the inevitable path down which queer theology leads, the unavoidable fruit that grows from the roots of "gay Christianity" (or, "gay Judaism"). As the Scriptures warned more than nineteen centuries ago, "But there were also false prophets among the people, even as there will be false teachers among you" (2 Peter 2:1). Need I say more?

*Edinburgh University has banned copies of the Bible from
student dormitories after condemning the Christian Union for violating
its "equality and diversity policy" by claiming that "any sexual activity
outside heterosexual marriage is not God-ordained."*

JONATHAN LUXMOORE,
"THE DAWKINS DELUSION: BRITAIN'S CRUSADING ATHEIST,"
COMMONWEAL 134, APRIL 20, 2007

*A Canadian professor has been fined two weeks' pay by a
Nova Scotia university for telling a student that homosexuality is an
unnatural lifestyle. . . . Cape Breton University (CBU) fined veteran
history professor David Mullan $2,100 in response to two human rights
complaints filed by a homosexual student who coordinates the campus'
Sexual Diversity Office. The student took umbrage at two letters the
professor had written to his former Anglican bishop two years ago.*

REPORTED BY *AGAPE PRESS*, JULY 26, 20062

*Ex-gay messages have no place in our nation's public schools.
A line has been drawn. There is no "other side" when you're
talking about lesbian, gay and bisexual students.*

KEVIN JENNINGS, FOUNDER OF GLSEN, *WASHINGTON TIMES*, JULY 27, 2004

*One reason I so dislike recent gay activism is that my self-identification
as a lesbian preceded Stonewall: I was the only openly gay person at the
Yale Graduate School (1968-72), a candor that was professionally costly.
That anyone with my aggressive and scandalous history could be
called "homophobic," as has repeatedly been done, shows just how
insanely Stalinist gay activism has become.*

CAMILLE PAGLIA, *VAMPS AND TRAMPS*

CHAPTER 5

Big Brother is Watching, and He Really Is Gay

The two teenage girls were terrified, having spent eighteen days in jail before appearing in court with shackles on their ankles, charged with a felony hate crime. When the judge announced that they could return home until their sentence was passed — meaning, confined to home detention with electronic monitoring — the girls sobbed uncontrollably. "Prosecutors eventually dropped the felony hate-crime charge in exchange for a plea bargain, in which the girls pleaded guilty to lesser misdemeanor charges of disorderly conduct and resisting arrest (the girls fled the scene when a police officer arrived; they did not strike an officer)."

They were eventually sentenced to one year of probation, forty hours of community service, and ordered to write letters of apology to the arresting officer and to a boy who was offended by their actions. And what exactly was their crime? Prof. Robert Gagnon tells the story:

In 2007 two 16-year old girls from Crystal Lake South High School (Ill.) were arrested on felony hate crime charges for distributing about 40 fliers on cars in the student parking lot of their high school. The fliers contained an anti-homosexual slur (the media have not reported what precisely the slur was) and a photo of two boys kissing, one of whom was identified as a classmate. The fliers contained no threats of violence. One of the girls was apparently getting back at a boy with whom she had once been best friend.

> … The girls told the court that the whole matter was a joke that they took too far. State Attorney Louis Bianchi told the press that he still felt the hate crime charge was justified, while acknowledging that the plea bargain was fair for juveniles.

And for this they were incarcerated for eighteen days in a juvenile detention center, shackled like dangerous criminals, and put on probation for one year.

To be sure, gay kids in school (along with kids perceived to be gay) have suffered more than enough harassment at the hands of their schoolmates, and to reiterate what we have said elsewhere in this book, there is no place for bullying and harassment in our schools. But in terms of the case at hand, the punishment hardly fits the crime — if it was really a crime at all.

According to some state officials, however, the girls most definitely committed a crime, and a hate crime at that:

> Assistant state's attorney for McHenry County, Thomas Carroll, commented: "You can be charged with a hate crime if you make a statement or take an action that inflicts injury or incites a breach of the peace based on a person's race, creed, gender, or perceived sexual orientation." Another assistant state's attorney, Robert Windon, said: "We do not feel this type of behavior is what the First Amendment protects." State's attorney Lou Bianchi insisted: "This is a classic case of the kind of conduct that the state legislature was directing the law against. This is what the legislators wanted to stop, this kind of activity."

Does anyone think that Carroll, Windon, and Bianchi would have reacted like this if the case involved anti-Christian flyers that were put on cars as opposed to anti-gay flyers, making fun of the faith of a Christian young man (be it done in jest or otherwise)? But such is the climate today that one of the worst accusations that can be brought against you is that you are anti-gay.

THE CONSEQUENCES OF USING THE NEW "F-" WORD

Just think of the almost hysterical reaction that followed the revelation that actor Isaiah Washington, star of ABC's *Grey's Anatomy*, referred to (then-closeted) gay co-star T. R. Knight with what is now called "the f- word" (meaning, faggot) during a heated, on-set incident. He then compounded his transgression by actually pronouncing the forbidden word in a backstage interview with reporters at the Golden Globes' event, held on Monday night, January 15th, 2007: "No, I did not call T.R a faggot. Never happened, never happened." Not only was he lying (apparently), but he actually mentioned the unmentionable word.

ABC was quick to express its outrage:

> "We are greatly dismayed that Mr. Washington chose to use such inappropriate language at the Golden Globes, language that he himself deemed 'unfortunate' in his previous public apology," the network said in a statement.

> "His actions are unacceptable and are being addressed," the statement concludes.

Neil Giuliano, president of GLAAD (the Gay & Lesbian Alliance Against Defamation) referred to the situation as "deeply troubling" and stated that Washington's repeated use of the word was "inexcusable," asking for a meeting to discuss "the destructive impact of these kinds of anti-gay slurs."

Then, on Thursday, January 18th, Washington came clean, expressing how deep his problems really were:

> In his apology Thursday, Washington acknowledged "repeating the word Monday night."

"I apologize to T.R., my colleagues, the fans of the show
and especially the lesbian and gay community for using a
word that is unacceptable in any context or circumstance. I
marred what should have been a perfect night for everyone
who works on 'Grey's Anatomy.' I can neither defend nor
explain my behavior. I can also no longer deny to myself
that there are issues I obviously need to examine within my
own soul, and I've asked for help."

He actually went for professional counseling and rehabilitation.
Despite his apology, however, and despite his efforts to make amends
with the GLBT community — not to mention his prominent role in
Grey's Anatomy — ABC fired him.

To be sure, it is inexcusable to slur someone with a word that
people find so offensive, just as it would be inexcusable for a white
person to use "the n-word" in referring to a black person. It's the
reaction here that is so extreme and is symptomatic of the larger, "Big
Brother Is Gay Syndrome."

Simply stated, since when does using an insulting word in the midst
of an angry argument call for an over-the-top apology like this: "I can
… no longer deny to myself that there are issues I obviously need to
examine within my own soul.…" Since when does it call for professional
counseling (to understand why he used "the f- word," as opposed to getting help with anger management)? People say and do stupid things all
the time, but when it comes to offending gays, a line of hyper-sensitivity
has been crossed. (To repeat yet again: I understand why there is such
sensitivity and I actively work to educate others about the struggles
endured by the GLBT community. I am simply highlighting the extreme
over-reaction to anything perceived as demeaning or offensive to gays.)

A DOUBLE STANDARD HERE?

But there's more. Within gay culture, "the f- word" has often been
used in self-description, most famously in Larry Kramer's 1978 novel
Faggots. Is one no longer allowed to refer to his book by name?

(Apparently, Naomi Wolf didn't think so, beginning her Foreword to Kramer's 2005 book, *The Tragedy of Today's Gays*, with these words: "Of course, I had heard of *Faggots*, growing up as I did in San Francisco in the 1970s....").

In 1999, Michael Thomas Ford, author of *Alec Baldwin Doesn't Love Me: And Other Trials from My Queer Life*, wrote his follow-up book entitled *That's Mr. Faggot to You: Further Trials from My Queer Life*. The positive review in *Publisher's Weekly* began by saying: "Cranky, bemused and extremely funny, Ford ... is brilliant even on potentially mundane topics like high school reunions ('Michael Thomas Ford is very proud to announce that he is still queer... [and] happier, more successful, and a great deal more attractive' than his former schoolmates')...."

Why wasn't *Publisher's Weekly* outraged by Ford's use of the forbidden word? Why could Ford use it so freely in 1999, but today, it can't even be uttered? And speaking of today, why was it OK for gay columnist Dan Savage to describe himself (and others of his ilk) as "radical sex-advice columnist faggots" on Keith Olbermann's TV show on January 4th, 2010? How dare he utter that word, even if, as he later explained, he was talking about the way he was viewed by conservative Christians? How could he be so glib? And was it right for him to turn the tables and, in a backhanded way, basically blame and malign Christians for his usage of the term?

And why is it acceptable for the GLBT community and its straight allies to bully their opponents if bullying is always wrong? As noted in a March 7, 2007, *Chicago Tribune* article, "Ellen Waltz, a Deerfield [IL] mother of eight, said the climate has changed so much that students who believe that homosexuality is immoral and violates their religious beliefs are now the ones being bullied."

Isaiah Washington's *faux pas* cost him his job and blemished his career. The error of the two high-school girls almost cost them their freedom — and we have barely begun to scratch the surface of the seismic shift that is taking place today.

Today, those who have come out of the closet are trying to put their ideological opponents into the closet; those preaching tolerance have become the most intolerant; those calling for inclusion are now the most exclusionary; those celebrating diversity demand absolute uniformity.

In the words of conservative gay journalist Charles Winecoff,

> Because gay is no longer taboo in America, the community has shifted its focus from supporting 'difference' to espousing a blanket Leftist agenda — in essence, suppressing diversity — and driving many of its own into a new (conservative) closet.

College professors have felt the heat of this repressive new order; researchers and scientists have encountered its ire; ministers have found themselves muzzled; teachers have been intimidated; employees have lost their jobs; even parents have been told they cannot exercise their rights. Queer has become something to fear, and gay is beginning to rule the day. The tables have been turned — dramatically. Who would have imagined?

Do you think I'm blowing things out of proportion? Do you think it's impossible that a tiny minority can have such a dominating influence over the great majority? The facts speak for themselves.

FAITH ORGANIZATIONS ARE LOSING THEIR RIGHTS

An April 9, 2009, article in the (certainly not conservative) *Washington Post* documented how "Faith organizations and individuals who view homosexuality as sinful and refuse to provide services to gay people are losing a growing number of legal battles that they say are costing them their religious freedom."

Correspondent Jacqueline L. Salmon cited these representative examples:

- A Christian photographer was forced by the New Mexico Civil Rights Commission to pay $6,637 in attorney's costs after she refused to photograph a gay couple's commitment ceremony.

- A psychologist in Georgia was fired after she declined for religious reasons to counsel a lesbian about her relationship.
- Christian fertility doctors in California who refused to artificially inseminate a lesbian patient were barred by the state Supreme Court from invoking their religious beliefs in refusing treatment.
- A Christian student group was not recognized at a University of California law school because it denies membership to anyone practicing sex outside of traditional marriage.

So much for freedom of conscience!

The article ended with this telling quote from Marc Stern, general counsel for the American Jewish Congress: "When you have a change that is as dramatic as has happened in the last 10 to 15 years with regards to attitudes toward homosexuality, it's inevitable it's going to reverberate in dozens of places in the law that you're never going to be able to foresee." In confirmation of this, Georgetown Law Professor Chai Feldblum, appointed by President Obama to serve on the U.S. Equal Employment Opportunity Commission, famously remarked that when push comes to shove, when religious liberty and sexual liberty conflict, "I'm having a hard time coming up with any case in which religious liberty should win." In more technical terms, she wrote, "Protecting one group's identity liberty may, at times, require that we burden others' belief liberties."

Writing in the *Washington Post* eighteen months later, political science professor Matthew J. Franck drew attention to other egregious cases, including:

> At [a] midwestern state university, a department chairman demurs from a student organizer's request that his department promote an upcoming "LGBTQ" film festival on campus; he is denounced to his university's chancellor, who indicates that his e-mail to the student warrants inquiry by a "Hate and Bias Incident Response Team."...

On a left-wing Web site, a petition drive succeeds in pres-
suring Apple to drop an "app" from its iTunes store for the
Manhattan Declaration, an ecumenical Christian statement
whose nearly half-million signers are united in defense of
the right to life, the tradition of conjugal marriage between
man and woman, and the principles of religious liberty. The
offense? The app is a "hate fest." Fewer than 8,000 people
petition for the app to go; more than five times as many
petition Apple for its reinstatement, so far to no avail.

Not only did the incident with the Manhattan Declaration expose
a glaring double standard within Apple (since numerous, sexually
explicit gay apps have not been removed, including apps with infor-
mation on gay bathhouses for anonymous sexual encounters, despite
complaints regarding their offensive content), but it also exposed the
mindset of gay activist groups (and their allies) that encouraged Apple
to remove the Manhattan Declaration app: All opposing views must
be silenced!

As expressed by the website that started the campaign to remove
the app:

> *Let's send a strong message to Apple that supporting
> homophobia and efforts to restrict choice [meaning, the
> "right" to abortion] is bad business.*

This was seconded by GLAAD (the Gay Lesbian Alliance Against
Defamation):

> Apple's action sent a powerful message that the company
> stands against intolerance.... Join GLAAD in thanking Apple
> for their action to remove the app and urging them to stay
> strong in the face of anti-gay activism.

So, if you support the institution of marriage as we have known it from the beginning of human history and if you dare take issue with the goals of gay activism, prepare to be censored — or worse.

"WHEN THE THOUGHT POLICE COME KNOCKING ON YOUR DOOR"

The really frightening thing is that it would be easy to write an entire book focusing on the subject matter of this chapter alone!

I could have cited scores of examples of universities in America and abroad where free speech is being shut down or muzzled, of employees losing their jobs because they took exception to gay activism in the work place, of educators being silenced for privately expressing their differences with homosexual practice, of Christian organizations being censured for holding to their convictions, and of religious leaders being silenced and harassed.

Space does not permit that, so I'll end here with the words of a children's play, produced by gay activists, followed by a warning from Australia. The play in question received widespread attention when Fox News picked up the story back in 2002. Here's the relevant background.

In October, 2001, Gray Davis, then governor of California, signed into law several bills that added "hate crimes" to the list of crimes included in "safe school" programs. Not long after this, a presentation called Cootie Shots was performed in many of the schools, involving children as young as seven (meaning, second graders).

> FOX News' William La Jeunesse reported: "Performed in hundreds of classes, 'Cootie Shots' include skits in which a transsexual boy says proudly, 'Let them say I'm a girl. What's wrong with being like a girl? Let them laugh, let them scream, they'll all be beheaded when I'm queen.' In another, a girl says, 'The one I love she wears a dress.' And in 'What's With the Dress, Jack?' Jack says, 'It shows off my legs.'"

"Let them laugh, let them scream, they'll all be beheaded when I'm queen." What a line! And seven-year-old kids were exposed to this?

To be sure, I don't expect to have my head chopped off for differing publicly with the goals of gay activism (after all, I have never accused gay activists of being jihadists or Taliban, among whom beheading is a common practice, although I have often been called those names by gay activists). But the day is not far off — in many respects, it is already here — when you and I can expect to be harassed or fired or interrogated or fined or jailed or attacked for actively holding to views like, "Marriage is the union of a man and woman only," or, "It's best for a child to be raised by his or her mother and father," or, "I believe that homosexual practice is wrong."

Recently, in Australia, Bill Muehlenberg addressed the consequences of a just-passed government policy, writing,

> Let me tell you in advance something you will need to know. If in the near future you notice that no new articles are being added to this website, and no new comments are being posted, there will be one very good reason for this: I will be in jail, or fighting a lengthy court battle, because of Victoria's new [Equal Opportunity Commission] law which was just passed.

According to this law, the government now has:

- The power to enter a church or meeting for the sole purpose of assessing what is said.
- The right to demand that a religious organisation hand over files.
- The right to compel church folk to attend a hearing at the Commission without any complaint being made.
- The power to initiate a complaint of discrimination.

Muehlenberg's column was appropriately entitled, "When the Thought Police Come Knocking on Your Door." You have been forewarned.

The Book the Publishers Were Afraid to Touch

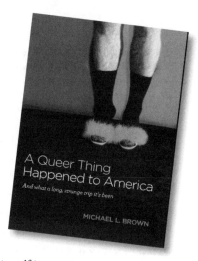

A Queer Thing
Happened to America
And what a long, strange trip it's been

MICHAEL L. BROWN

FROM A CONSERVATIVE PUNDIT:

"Book publishing is a difficult business now, and no media is willing to promote a book that opposes homosexuality.... Economic self-interest is going to make it very tough for a publisher to say yes."

FROM A CONSERVATIVE PUBLISHER:

"There would be a very concrete, though difficult to measure financial penalty to pay for publishing your book.... Practically speaking it could actually destroy the firm..."

FROM A BESTSELLING CONSERVATIVE AUTHOR:

"Honestly, there is no NY publisher...who will touch this manuscript."

FROM THE HEAD OF A NEW YORK CITY PUBLICITY FIRM:

"Unfortunately [he] spoke with his team and he doesn't have anyone willing to take on Dr. Brown's book."

FROM A PUBLISHING INSIDER:

"I'd be better off burning the money in my fireplace.... The economics of publishing a book like this are bleak."

FROM A TOP LITERARY AGENT WHO FARMED THE MANUSCRIPT OUT TO A NUMBER OF LEADING PUBLISHERS:

"Most thought the material was too controversial…all felt that the title would need to be changed.

Forty years ago, most Americans said they didn't know anyone who was homosexual and claimed to know little or nothing about homosexuality. Today, there's hardly a sitcom without a prominent gay character, movies like *Milk* and *Brokeback Mountain* have won Oscars, and even *People* magazine celebrated the marriage of Ellen Degeneres and Portia DeRossi. *A Queer Thing Happened to America* chronicles the amazing transformation of America over the last forty years, and addresses the question head-on: Is there really a gay agenda, or is it a fiction of the religious right? Written in a lively and compelling style, but backed with massive research and extensive interaction with the GLBT community, this forthright and yet compassionate book looks at the extraordinary impact gay activism has had on American society. This could easily be the most controversial book of the decade. Read it and find out why the publishing world was afraid to touch it.